Questions Asked

Questions Asked

JOSTEIN GAARDER

Illustrations by Akin Duzakın

Translation from Norwegian by Don Bartlett

Where does the world come from?
Has there always been something
here? Or has it all come from
nothing?

Is our planet the only one with life on it?
Or is the universe teeming with life?

Could all the stars and planets have been here without anyone knowing about them?

Are there other clever creatures like us in the universe? Could there be creatures out there who have a better understanding of the world than we do?

Do angels and ghosts exist?
Has anyone ever seen a
supernatural being?

Can anyone know what I think?

How do my legs go where I want
them to go while my mind is
elsewhere?

Is it possible to be afraid without
knowing what you are afraid of ?

What do I fear losing most?

How can I remember things that happened a long time ago? Why do I forget some things? How is it that I can suddenly remember them again?

What is time? When something is past, is it gone forever?

Can anyone do real magic tricks?

Do miracles happen sometimes?

Do I need to have lots of possessions
to be happy?

Can I be sure that all my memories
really happened?

Is it possible to exist and not think about anything at all?

What will the world be like in a
hundred years? What will it be like
here in a thousand years? Or in a
hundred thousand years? Will there
be people living on Earth then?

Did a god create us? Or did we create our own ideas of a god in our minds?

Can those who are not with us any
more know how we are?

Why am I alive? Why does
the world exist? Why is there
anything at all?

Twins can be like two drops of water.
Can two minds be the same?

Can I love another person as I
love myself ?

How do I talk? How do I find
the exact words I need from all the
words in my head?

Why do I dream? What goes on
in my head when I'm asleep?

Are experiences more real when I'm awake than when I'm dreaming?

What happens when I die? Could I
wake up in another reality?

What is a good friend? Can an animal be my best friend?

What are the most important
things in life?

What will my life be like?

What shall I do with my life?

JOSTEIN GAARDER is the author of several novels, short stories, and children's books. His best known work is the novel *Sophie's World: A Novel About the History of Philosophy* (1991). It has been translated into 60 languages. He lives in Oslo, Norway with his family.

AKIN DÜZAKIN is a Turkish-Norwegian illustrator and children's author. He received the Brage Prize in 1995 and 1997, the Unni Sands bildebokpris in 1998, and the Bokkunstprisen in 2006.

DON BARTLETT has translated novels by many Danish and Norwegian authors, among them Per Petterson, Roy Jacobsen, Ida Jessen, Jo Nesbø, and Gunnar Staalesen. He is the translator of Karl Ove Knausgaard's *My Struggle* series. He lives with his family in Norfolk, England.

First Elsewhere Editions Printing, 2017

Library of Congress Cataloging-in-Publication Data
Questions Asked / Jostein Gaarder; illustrations by Akin Düzakin ;
translation from Norwegian by Don Bartlett.
Other titles: Det Spørs. English
LCCN 2016025199 (print) | LCCN 2016041803 (ebook)
ISBN: 9780914671664 (hardback)
ISBN 9780914671671 (E-book)

Elsewhere Editions
232 3rd Street #A111
Brooklyn, NY 11215

Distributed by Penguin Random House
www.penguinrandomhouse.com

This publication was made possible with support from the Lannan Foundation,
the Amazon Literary Partnership, the Nimick Forbesway Foundation,
the National Endowment for the Arts,
the New York State Council on the Arts, a state agency,
and the New York City Department of Cultural Affairs.

PRINTED IN CHINA